Garfield
The Complete Cat Book

**Based on the
character created by
Jim Davis**

Random House • New York

Acknowledgments

Thomas Y. Crowell, Publishers: Text of "Half Asleep" and "Your Cat and Mine" from MY CAT HAS EYES OF SAPPHIRE BLUE by Aileen Fisher. Copyright © 1973 by Aileen Fisher. By permission of Thomas Y. Crowell, Publishers.

Doubleday & Company, Inc., and A. P. Watt & Son: "The Cat That Walked by Himself," copyright 1902 by Rudyard Kipling from RUDYARD KIPLING'S VERSE: DEFINITIVE EDITION. Reprinted by permission of the National Trust of Great Britain, Doubleday & Company, Inc., A. P. Watt & Son, and Macmillan London Ltd.

Eleanor Farjeon: "Cats" from THE CHILDREN'S BELLS by Eleanor Farjeon (Oxford University Press). Reprinted by permission.

Little, Brown and Company and Curtis Brown, Ltd.: "The Kitten" from VERSES FROM 1929 ON by Ogden Nash. Copyright 1940 by The Curtis Publishing Company. First appeared in *The Saturday Evening Post.* Reprinted by permission of Little, Brown and Company and Curtis Brown, Ltd.

Eve Merriam: "What in the World" from THERE IS NO RHYME FOR SILVER by Eve Merriam. Copyright © 1962 by Eve Merriam. Reprinted by permission of the author.

William Morrow & Company, Inc.: "Alley Cat School" from CITY SANDWICH by Frank Asch. Copyright © 1978 by Frank Asch. Reprinted by permission of Greenwillow Books (A Division of William Morrow & Company).

Frederick Warne & Company, Inc.: "Squatter's Rights" by Richard Shaw from THE CAT BOOK. Copyright © 1973 by Frederick Warne & Company, Inc. Reproduced by permission of Frederick Warne & Company, Inc.

Written by Shep Steneman
Typography by Charlotte Staub

Photograph Credits: Page 2—© Terry De Roy Gruber; 3—© Walter Chandoha; 4—© Walter Chandoha; 5—© Walter Chandoha; 6—© Walter Chandoha; 7—© Walter Chandoha; 8—© Paula Wright/Animals, Animals; 9—© Walter Chandoha; 10—© Alice Su; 11—The Metropolitan Museum of Art, Purchase, 1958; 12—William Rockhill Nelson Gallery of Art; 13—The Metropolitan Museum of Art, Gift in memory of Charles Stewart Smith, 1914; 14—Courtesy, Alan Forman; 15—© Mary Eleanor Browning/Photo Researchers, Inc.; 16—© Walter Chandoha; 17—(top) © Cindy Kreider/Taurus Photos, (bottom) © George F. Godfrey/Animals, Animals; 18—(top) © Walter Chandoha, (bottom) © Crezentia Allen; 19—(top left) © Mary Eleanor Browning/National Audubon Society/Photo Researchers, Inc., (top right & bottom) © Crezentia Allen; 20—(top) © Terence A. Gili/Animals, Animals, (center & bottom) © Crezentia Allen; 21—(top) © Jane Howard/Photo Researchers, Inc., (bottom) © Crezentia Allen; 22—(top) © Crezentia Allen, (center) © Walter Chandoha, (bottom) © Terence A. Gili/Animals, Animals; 23—(top) © Crezentia Allen, (bottom) © Walter Chandoha; 24—(top) © Norman Hecker, (bottom) © Crezentia Allen; 25—(top) © Jeanne White/National Audubon Society/Photo Researchers, Inc., (bottom) © Crezentia Allen; 26—(top) © Crezentia Allen, (bottom) © Mary Eleanor Browning/National Audubon Society/Photo Researchers, Inc.; 27—(top) © Crezentia Allen, (bottom) © Ray Hoyt; 28—© Ylla 1976/Photo Researchers, Inc.; 29—(top) Crezentia Allen, (bottom) Terry De Roy Gruber; 30—© Terry De Roy Gruber; 31—© Ylla/Rapho/Photo Researchers, Inc.; 32—© Walter Chandoha; 33—© Terry De Roy Gruber; 35—© Bill Strode 1980/Woodfin Camp & Assoc.; 36—© Terry De Roy Gruber; 37—© Walter Chandoha; 39—© Michael P. Gadomski/Bruce Coleman, Inc.; 41—© Walter Chandoha; 43—© Lawrence Frank 1976; 44—© Joe Munroe 1976/National Audubon Society/Photo Researchers, Inc.; 46—© Terry De Roy Gruber; 48—© Walter Chandoha; 49—The Granger Collection; 50—© Mary Eleanor Browning/Photo Researchers, Inc.; 51—UPI; 53—Courtesy, Star-Kist; 54-55—© Terry De Roy Gruber; 59—UPI; 60—© Terry De Roy Gruber; 61—(top) Jean Poulos/Courtesy, Surfer Magazine, (bottom) Syndication International; 65—© Walter Chandoha; 66—(left) New York Public Library, Picture Collection, (right) The Metropolitan Museum of Art, The Jules S. Bache Collection, 1949; 67—(left) The National Gallery of Art, Washington, D.C., (top right) New York Public Library, Picture Collection, (bottom right) The Metropolitan Museum of Art, The Smith Collection, Gift in memory of Charles Stewart Smith, 1914; 68—(top) New York Public Library, Picture Collection, (bottom) The National Gallery of Art, Washington, D.C., Gift of Edgar William and Bernice Chrysler Garbisch; 69—(top) New York Public Library, Picture Collection, (bottom) The Metropolitan Museum of Art, Rogers Fund, 1922; 70—© Monique Manceau/Photo Researchers, Inc.; 71—(top) © Jook Leung/Taurus Photos, (bottom) © Spencer Carter 1981/Woodfin Camp & Assoc.; 72-73—New York Public Library, Picture Collection; 74—© Leonard Speier; 75—© Mary Eleanor Browning/National Audubon Society/Photo Researchers, Inc.; 76—Russ Kinne/Photo Researchers, Inc.; 78—New York Public Library, Picture Collection; 79—New York Public Library, Picture Collection; 80—© Walter Chandoha; 81—© David "Chim" Seymour/ICP; 84—The Granger Collection; 85—© Karen Tweedy-Holmes/Animals, Animals; 86—© Ylla/Rapho/Photo Researchers, Inc.; 87—© Jane Howard 1975/Photo Researchers.

Library of Congress Cataloging in Publication Data: Steneman, Shep. Garfield's complete cat book. Bibliography: p. 88.
SUMMARY: Explores the world of cats, including their history, characteristics, occupations, myths, and a few feline secrets.
   1. Cats—Juvenile literature. [1. Cats] I. Davis, Jim. II. Title.
SF445.7.S74   636.8 81-50246   ISBN 0-394-84893-4 (trade); 0-394-94893-9 (lib. bdg.) AACR2

Manufactured in the United States of America
2 3 4 5 6 7 8 9 0

Contents

 *Introduction*

In this book you'll find answers to all sorts of questions about cats. You'll learn why a cat has whiskers and how a cat talks to you with its tail! You'll meet cats who work and cats who never lift a paw.

As Garfield will tell you, cats are warm, cuddly, affectionate, handsome, and lovable—but they are also *very* independent.

The Complete Cat Book will explain a lot of the cat's secrets to you, but not *all* of them. Garfield and his feline friends would never stand for that!

The Basic Cat

Cats and people have a lot in common. Like us, cats are mammals—warm-blooded animals covered with hair. They nourish their young with milk, as we do, and have some of the same features: hearts, stomachs, bones, and teeth. Cats eat some of the same food we eat and catch some of the same diseases. Cats act a lot like people too, with every kind of mood: happy, sleepy, playful—devilish!

But a quick look in the mirror will tell you—and your cat—that you are also very different. Domestic cats like Garfield belong to the larger cat family, including lions, tigers, leopards, and pumas. All the cats are *carnivores* (CAR-nuh-vorz)—animals that survive by hunting and killing other animals.

Lions are the only cats who live in groups. All the others are solitary creatures, living and hunting alone, marking off special territories to defend against enemies. The domestic cats in our homes still have many traits of their wild ancestors—just watch a kitten stalk a ball of yarn!

The cat's body is very flexible because it includes 244 bones and many muscles. Watch a cat grooming: it bends and twists like a pretzel! There *is* one place where the cat can't reach: a small area right behind the head. That's why cats love being scratched there.

A cat's furry body insulates it against extreme heat or cold. When a cat gets angry or scared, tiny muscles under the skin cause its hair to stand on end. This makes the cat look a lot bigger—big enough to scare away an enemy. Cat fur seems electric too. It crackles when you brush it in cold weather, and if you rub it at night, it sparks!

2

When a cat walks, its front legs swing inward toward its body. This explains why cats can balance so gracefully on narrow fences and mantelpieces. The soles of the cat's feet are protected by tough pads. The cat's claws are covered by folds of skin as it walks. This keeps the claws from making any noise that could scare its prey away. When it wants to, the cat can bare its claws—in a flash!

Some people are afraid of cats because of their claws. But don't be! Cats use their claws only for hunting small animals and defending themselves against bigger ones.

They use their claws against people only if it's necessary to defend themselves.

If a cat falls, it has a special "righting reflex" that lets it twist around in midair and land on its feet. But cats can still be seriously hurt if they fall too far. Cats sense this, and if they climb too high in a tree, they won't budge! If nobody rescues them, though, cats will eventually climb down—backward.

The cat's teeth cut like pinking shears, grasping and tearing food instead of chewing it. When a cat licks you, its tongue feels rough. What you feel are the tiny barbs that help the cat scrape meat from bones or pull loose fur from its coat. The tongue also curls into a clever spoon shape for lapping liquids.

Most people think cats can see in total darkness. They can't. But they *can* see in very dim light—even on a night with no moon and just a few stars. When a cat's sensitive eyes reflect light, they *glow*, giving them that fascinating spooky look! During the day your cat's eyes may be green, but at night the black irises open very wide to let in more light—and then the black irises make your cat's eyes look *black*!

Cats can see colors, but seeing color isn't as important to them as seeing movement—like the quick skittering of a mouse. Cats often sit patiently, staring into space, waiting for something to scurry by. When something does, they spot it instantly and are off and running!

A cat hears high-pitched sounds that

we can't hear. When it needs to pinpoint the exact location, it keeps its head still and swivels its ears. No human being can do that.

Cats make at least sixteen different sounds themselves, everything from a welcoming *chirrrup* to a high-pitched yelp. They can also produce a pathetic meow, a scared squawk, and a terrifying HISSSSSS!

The cat's purr probably comes from two folds of tissue called the false vocal cords. We still aren't really sure about how cats purr. But we do know they purr when they're well-fed and contented. They also have a special purr if they're very sick or in pain.

Cats' hair and skin are very sensitive, and their whiskers are the most sensitive of all. Cats' whiskers guide them through dark places and help them feel the shapes of objects too close for their eyes to focus on. Of course, it's also true that cats wouldn't be half as handsome without their whiskers! How else can a cat surprise you with a friendly tickle?

Cats don't use their sense of smell for finding prey, but they recognize other cats with it. They rub their own scent glands on trees, leaving a smell that's a warning: "This is *my* territory. All other cats stay away!" So if your cat nuzzles you with its chin (where a scent gland is) he's saying, "You belong to me!"

POOMP!!

Body language is very important to cats. When a cat is threatened, it can do several different things. Sometimes it faces its enemy and hisses, ready to charge! Or it might stand sideways, arching its back and bristling its fur to look bigger. A cat that knows it's outmatched will flatten down against the ground, growling and baring its teeth. Then, if absolutely necessary, it can roll over quickly and claw its attacker.

You can read a cat's mind by watching its tail. When a walking cat carries its tail high like a banner, it's calm and content (and proud of itself!). An angry cat thrashes its tail wildly. A bristling tail means the cat feels threatened. A tail extended straight out behind means that

the cat's about to attack. Just before a cat pounces it stays very still. Nothing moves—except for a tiny twitching at the tip of its tail!

Cats are very clean animals. They wash their faces and paws after every meal. And they give the rest of their bodies frequent baths with their rough, washcloth tongues. Their grooming also stimulates glands that keep their coats waterproof. In warm weather their saliva acts like sweat, cooling off their fur.

Sometimes cats groom to avoid responding to a scold or a threat. Sometimes they groom when they're scared. As Paul Gallico wrote, the cat's motto could well be, When in doubt, wash.

Kittens

Kittens are born about sixty-three days after their parents have mated. The mother cat uses her raspy tongue to lick off the transparent sac around each kitten. Then the kitten can breathe. The mother also licks the kitten's fur until it's clean and dry.

Most mother cats have four kittens in a litter, but some have given birth to as many as fourteen at one time!

Newborn kittens are blind for the first two weeks. They find their mother by hearing, touching, and smelling her. Each kitten chooses one of its mother's eight nipples as its own personal milk supply. The kitten keeps the milk flowing by pressing its paws back and forth—kneading—against its mother's belly. Adult cats often remember this old soothing motion and do it when they're contentedly lying on something soft and warm—like you!

Kittens get their baby teeth about the same time they open their eyes. At about three or four weeks kittens start playing. They run, chase, leap, pounce, and fight! This is useful training for cats who will have to hunt.

The cat's mother teaches her kittens

> *Like humans, cats have two sets of teeth. The average kitten has twenty-six baby teeth until it's about six months old. The average adult cat has thirty teeth.*

how to eat solid food and shows them how to use a litter box. She even gives them mice-catching lessons. A cat who has never been taught by its mother will never know how to catch mice—though it will certainly try. By the time a kitten is eight weeks old, it's ready to leave its mother and start life in a new home.

There's no sure way to say how long a cat will live. Abandoned cats in the wild are likely to die young. Cats who roam have shorter lives than cats who stay indoors. Some cats who are well-cared for can live to be seventeen. Many, many cats have lived twenty years and some have made it to thirty. A cat in Europe had kittens at the age of twenty-six!

Cat History

No one is sure when or where wild cats were domesticated. We do know that about four thousand years ago the ancient Egyptians kept cats in their homes.

The Egyptians first kept cats to hunt the rats and mice that were eating their grain. But eventually something about the cat—its crescent-moonlike circle when sleeping, its ability to see in the dark, or its strong gaze, which seems to see right through you—made the Egyptians decide that the cat must be related to the gods. They began worshiping cats and had a cat goddess named Bastet. She was also known as Bast or Pasht. (Our word "puss" comes from the word "pasht.")

Bastet was goddess of the sun, moon, love, and fertility. Statues usually show her with a cat's head and a human body. Over five hundred thousand people traveled each spring to Bastet's temple to celebrate a joyous festival. They sang and drank and danced. Women outlined their eyes in dark colors to look like cats.

Cats lived like kings in ancient Egypt. House pets were fed fresh fish and bread soaked in milk. They often ate from their masters' plates. A cat in a wealthy home was given a gold or jeweled collar to wear. Craftsmen showed their love for cats by making everything from huge bronze statues of cats for temples to tiny ornaments of them for necklaces and bracelets. There are paintings of cats hunting with people and sitting under the chairs of their owners. If anyone killed a cat in Egypt, he was sentenced to death!

Cats owned by wealthy families also had expensive funerals. The family members shaved off their eyebrows as a sign of mourning. Then an embalmer treated the cat with drugs and spices and wrapped it in colorful strips of linen. A mask was put on its face and a jeweled collar around its neck. Then the body was placed in a brightly decorated

Japanese good-luck statue

10

GARFIELD'S HISTORY OF CATS: THE FIRST CAT WAS DOMESTICATED ABOUT A MILLION YEARS AGO. THE CAT (NAMED "ORG") WAS OWNED BY A CAVE MAN NAMED "CHUCK"

WHILE RUMOR HAS IT THAT ORG ATE HIS OWNER...

HISTORIANS MAINTAIN THE FAMILY DOG ATE CHUCK

mummy case and buried in a special cemetery. To be sure the cat wasn't hungry in its afterlife, mouse mummies were buried with it.

In death or life, ancient Egypt was a great place to be a cat!

There *was* one time when the Egyptians' love for cats got them into trouble. When a Persian army attacked an Egyptian city, each of the Persian soldiers carried a live cat. The Egyptians refused to harm the sacred animals and immediately surrendered.

It was illegal to take cats out of Egypt, but some were smuggled out. Greece sent spies to Egypt to steal cats, and Egypt sent spies to Greece to bring them back! The Greeks and Romans admired cats for their usefulness, but they didn't treat them as gods.

Egyptian sculpture of Bastet, cat goddess

A king of Wales named Howell the Good included cats in his laws. A blind kitten was said to be worth one penny. When it opened its eyes, its value went up to twopence. After it killed its first mouse, the cat was worth fourpence. In those days a penny went very far. It could buy a lamb, a goose, or a hen.

In China cats were admired as hunters. But in Japan they were treasured for their beauty. The Japanese pampered their cats and kept them on leashes. Members of the Imperial Court were the only people allowed to own them. In the thirteenth century rats and mice started eating Japanese grain and silkworms. To solve the problem the government ordered all the cats set free. And it worked! The cats saved the silk and the grain harvests.

Cats were treated well in Moslem countries too. When the great prophet Mohammed was called to prayers one day, he noticed his cat, Muezza, sleeping on the sleeve of his robe. Rather than disturb the cat, Mohammed cut off his sleeve.

In the thirteenth century a Moslem sultan willed the income from his orchard to the needy cats of Cairo. For hundreds of years afterward street cats were treated daily to a free meal.

In the Dark Ages European cats were treated poorly and were considered by some people to be agents of the Devil. But little by little cats began to return to human favor. Members of royal courts

Japanese sculpture

fussed over them, and artists put cats in their paintings.

Around the turn of the century humane societies were formed to protect all domestic animals from cruelty. Today, of course, the cat is one of our favorite animals, and it seems to be getting more popular all the time.

Japanese painting

Cat Breeds

Most house cats are mixtures of two or more different breeds. They may be silver, blue, brown, black, red, white, or a combination of many colors. Cats born in the same litter are often different colors. Some may have short hair and some may have long hair.

But over the years cat breeders have singled out cats they think are extremely beautiful or unusual and have purposely bred them to maintain their traits.

Today there are more than twenty recognized cat breeds. Some have evolved naturally over hundreds of years. Others have been developed by breeders.

The Cat Fancy—organizers of cat clubs and shows—has determined specific standards for all the cat breeds. For ex-

---

Certificate of Pedigree

Fabulous Felines, Inc. TM

Name GRETA
Breed RUSSIAN BLUE
Color BLUE
Color of Eyes GREEN
Date of Birth SEPTEMBER 16, 0978
Sex FEMALE

Grand Parents:

Sire:

SILVER SWEET II

TRIPLE CHAMPION HY-LINES SILVER SON OF SANNA MARS

CHAMPION HY-LINES BLU SONNET OF SANNA MARS

Dam:

QUAD. CHAMPION SANNA-MARS SILVER SILVIA

TRIPLE CHAMPION HY-LINES SILVER SON OF SANNA MARS

CHAMPION HY-LINES BLU SONNET OF SANNA MARS

Great Grand Parents:

GRAND CHAMPION HY-LINES SILVER CLOUD

GRANDCHAMPION VELVAS SILVER QUEEN OF HY-LINE

GRAND CHAMPION HY-LINES SILVER KNIGHT

CHAMPION HY-LINES SILVER PRINCESS

GRAND CHAMPION HY-LINES SILVER CLOUD

GRAND CHAMPION VELVAS SILVER QUEEN OF HY-LINE

GRAND CHAMPION HY-LINES SILVER KNIGHT

CHAMPION HY-LINES SILVER PRINCESS

Owner of the Above Described Cat

ALAN FORMAN

Address 845 EAST 33rd STREET
NEW YORK, N.Y.

I HEREBY CERTIFY that, to the best of my knowledge and belief, the above pedigree is true and that all ancestors named above are of the same breed unless otherwise noted.

Signed this 22nd *day of* MAY 19 70

FABULOUS FELINES, INC., 133 LEXINGTON AVENUE, NEW YORK, N.Y. 10016

ample, the standard for the Russian Blue says it must have green eyes, a light-blue coat, and no white hairs anywhere. There are also standards for ideal body shape— head, neck, legs, paws, and nose. Cat show judges give the highest scores to the cats that come closest to the standards.

These organizations also register pure-bred cats. A registered cat comes with official papers that show its pedigree— each ancestor as far back as its sixteen great-great-grandparents!

Cat fanciers use special terms to describe cats. Here are a few important ones:

Points   The "points" of a cat are dark areas of color on the face, paws, ears, and tail of some breeds, like the Siamese. In America the Siamese is bred in four types: from darkest to lightest they are seal point, chocolate point, blue point, and lilac point.

Tabby Cats with patterned markings are called tabbies. The striped or mackerel tabby has stripes down the sides of its body. The classic tabby has swirling patterns that look like blotches or bull's-eyes. In both breeds, dark lines form the letter "M" on the forehead. Could it stand for "meow"?

***Calico and Tortoise-
shell*** The calico is white
with black and reddish-orange
patches and mostly white on
its legs and chest. The tor-
toiseshell is mostly black with
patches of reddish-orange or
white. Most calicos and tor-
toiseshells are females.

Shorthair Cats

Abyssinian

Experts say that the playful Abyssinian looks like the sacred cat of ancient Egypt. The first one in England did come from a country near Egypt called Ethiopia (once known as Abyssinia), but it's not certain the breed really began there. Abyssinians, nicknamed Abys, have reddish-brown hair-ticked coats. "Hair-ticked" means that each hair is tipped in dark brown or black. Abys are friendly and active—always ready for fun!

Bombay

The Bombay, a cross between the Shorthair and the Burmese, is a new variety too. What's special about the Bombay is its coat: fine short hairs of jet black with a "patent leather" sheen.

American Shorthair

The American Shorthair is an all-American cat, and some of its ancestors may have come over on the *Mayflower.* American Shorthairs are smart and friendly, and their muscular legs make them excellent hunters. These cats come in every possible pattern and color combination!

American Wirehair

The American Wirehair sprang up by mutation in the 1960s. It's very much like the American Shorthair, but its fur is stiff and wiry to the touch.

British Shorthair

The British Shorthair is more compact than its American cousin. It has a broad head and a short, dense coat. It's bred in seventeen colors and patterns. The British Shorthair is very sociable with children—and dogs!

Burmese

The first Burmese cat to appear in the United States was a female named Wong Mau who was brought here with a sailor in 1930. She had a glossy brown coat, but other colors have been developed since then. The Burmese is sturdy and muscular and is extremely affectionate with people.

Colorpoint Shorthair

Colorpoint Shorthairs are identical to Siamese except in color. They were bred by mating Siamese cats with the American Shorthair. They have the Siamese body lines and points but are bred in a wider variety of colors and patterns. Some are especially valued for their deep electric-blue eyes.

Egyptian Mau

Mau is the ancient Egyptian word for cat. It certainly sounds like what cats say! The Mau is the only domestic spotted cat. It looks like the cats in ancient Egyptian artwork. Maus in America are all descended from two cats brought over from Cairo. They come in color mixtures of silver, bronze, and smoke.

Exotic Shorthair

Breeders created the Exotic Shorthair by mating shorthairs with Persians. It's just like the Persian but has a shorter coat—perfect for people who like Persians but hate to groom their long hair.

Havana Brown

The Havana Brown's name comes from its tobacco-colored coat—the same shade as Havana cigars. But the Havana Brown didn't come from Cuba. It's descended from Siamese, Russian Blue, and other shorthairs. Havana Browns have a rich brown coat, brown skin, brown nose—and brown whiskers!

Japanese Bobtail

The Bobtail arrived in America in 1969. It has lived in Japan for hundreds of years, where it's called Mi-Ke (MEE-Kay). It has a three-colored coat, and the Japanese people feel that it brings them good luck. The short tail looks like a pompon or a rabbit's tail.

Korat

People in Thailand think the Korat, a muscular, green-eyed cat, brings them good luck. It's known there as Si-Sawat, a reference to its striking silver-blue coat. True Korats are rare, even in Thailand, and they're also very rare among American cat fanciers.

Manx

The Manx is named for the Isle of Man, a small island off the coast of England. Most Manxes don't have tails, but all Manx cats have a thick, soft undercoat and a glossy outer coat resembling rabbit fur. The Manx's long hind legs give it a bunnylike walk. Is it a cross between a rabbit and a cat? NO!

Oriental Shorthair

Oriental Shorthairs were specially bred to preserve the elegant Siamese body line, but in a variety of solid colors—blue, red, and lavender. They don't have the Siamese points, but some of them have tabby patterns.

Rex

Some dogs are called Rex, and some cats are too! The first Rex cat was a curly-coated mutation named Kallibunker. He was found near Cornwall, England, in 1950 and was mated to his mother to produce more curly-coated cats. Today every Rex cat in Cornwall is descended from Kallibunker. Rex cats have also turned up in other countries. They have large ears and crinkled whiskers to match their curly hair. The Rex has only an undercoat, so it doesn't shed. If you are allergic to cat hair you may not be allergic to the Rex.

Russian Blue

The Russian Blue probably first came from the far northern Russian port of Archangel. It has a short, thick, blue coat that makes it comfortable in cold climates. You can trace pictures in its thick fur with your finger. Queen Victoria owned a Russian Blue.

Scottish Fold

No, it's not a dance—it's a cat! A mutation named Susie was born in 1961 on a farm in Scotland, and all Scottish Fold cats are descended from her. The ears of this breed are folded down and forward to make it look different from any other cat. Its colors and patterns are like the British Shorthair's.

Siamese

According to legend Siamese cats first belonged to the King of Siam (the former name of Thailand) and were trained to guard the palace walls. The first Siamese cats in America were gifts from the King of Siam in the late 1800s. Today there are more Siamese cats in America than in Thailand.

Siamese cats have sleek lines, handsome points, and loud, insistent voices. Some Siamese are cross-eyed or kinky-tailed, which makes them poor scorers at cat shows. Siamese are the most talkative cats you can own!

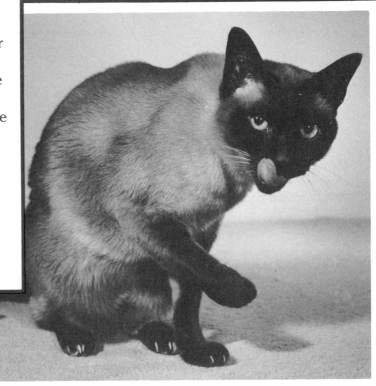

Somali

This is a long-haired version of the Abyssinian, but it's still considered a shorthair. The special "ticking" of the coat can take months to develop.

Longhair Cats

Balinese

The Balinese looks like a Siamese but has a long, silky coat. It does *not* come from the island of Bali. The breeders named it Balinese because they said it looked as graceful and beautiful as a Balinese dancer.

Birman

The Birman is called the Sacred Cat of Burma, though it's not related to the short-haired Burmese. Birmans are easier to groom than other longhairs because their fur doesn't tangle. They look very dapper with their "white gloved" paws.

Himalayan

The Himalayan is a long-haired cat, like the Persian, but has the colors and points of a Siamese. The Himalayan's voice is gentle. Kittens are cream-colored when they're born; the points darken as they get older. The Himalayan got its name because its fur looks like the coat of the Himalayan rabbit.

Maine Coon Cat

The Maine Coon is one of the biggest and heaviest cats. It was first seen in Maine in the 1850s. The sturdy, muscular body and thick shaggy coat keep the Maine Coon comfortable throughout the coldest Maine winter. Because of its markings and large paws, it was mistakenly thought to be the result of mating cats with raccoons!

Persian

Persian cats probably came from Iran (once known as Persia). They have broad heads, large, round eyes, and long, glossy coats. Persians can be white, red, cream, blue, or black as well as patterned. There is a special Persian called the Peke-Face, whose head resembles the face of a Pekinese dog. Persians are calm and good-natured even though they look so snobbish—preening and showing off their beauty! If you own a Persian, be prepared to brush its long fur *every* day.

Turkish Angora

The Angora comes from Turkey, and its name is probably a misspelling of the Turkish city of Ankara. When it walks, it carries its long, full tail forward, almost brushing its head. It looks like it's saluting! Only pure-white Angora cats are eligible for cat shows.

A Hairless Cat

Sphinx

The Sphinx is the only cat without hair. It doesn't even have whiskers, but it does have some fuzzy down on its head and chest. Because it lacks a coat, the Sphinx should usually live indoors. The Sphinx may be a good cat for you if you are allergic to other felines.

Choosing a Cat

It's great fun choosing a cat! And there are different ways to do it. You can adopt one from an animal shelter. This is a wonderful thing to do because it often saves an animal's life. You can buy a cat from a breeder or be given one by a friend whose cat has had kittens. Sometimes a stray cat will adopt *you*! Before you decide to get a cat, ask yourself a few questions.

Do you really want a cat?

Cats aren't expensive to care for, but food and litter do cost money, and so do visits to the veterinarian. Are you allergic to cats? If you are, then having a cat around might make you sneeze all day long!

Will you take care of your cat?

Your cat has to be fed and given water every day. And it needs a clean litter box too. These chores don't take very much time, but they can't be ignored. There *is* one especially nice thing about owning a cat: you don't have to walk it in cold, wintry weather!

Do you want a kitten or a cat?

Kittens need more attention and training than older cats do. They are also delicate. A very young child should *never* be given a kitten, because the child would treat it much too roughly.

Kittens generally adapt to a new home easier than adult cats do. If you already have other pets, a kitten will fit itself in with them. An adult cat may not.

The Kitten

The Trouble with a Kitten is THAT Eventually it becomes a CAT.

—Ogden Nash,
Verses from 1929 On

Most people like to train kittens and watch them grow—wishing they would stay kittens longer! But a friendly, affectionate, grown cat can also come into your home—and your heart. The choice is up to you!

Should your cat be registered?

If you want a rare kind of cat—say, a black cat without a *single* white hair, or a cat that wins championships at shows, you'll need to get a registered pedigreed. These cats have papers tracing their ancestors back at least four generations. Pedigreed cats are usually expensive.

Most of the millions of cats in the world *aren't* registered. Their owners don't care if they can't trace back their cats' families. As pets, their cats are just as loving and playful —and handsome too! They also cost a lot less.

Should your cat have long or short hair?

Long-haired cats need special attention. They have to be brushed every day to keep their coats from matting and tangling. Long-haired cats love being brushed—but you might find it a chore!

Your Cat and Mine

My cat has eyes
of sapphire blue.
Your cat has eyes of green.
My cat is of a
buffy hue,
and yours has tiger-sheen.
And you tell me,
and I tell you:
"My cat is better
through and through
than any cat I've seen."

—Aileen Fisher,
My Cat Has Eyes of Sapphire Blue

Should your cat be male or female?

Males and females make excellent pets. Both are friendly and affectionate. Each cat has its own personality, which generally has nothing to do with its sex.

Male cats spray their surroundings with bad-smelling urine to mark their territory. Females can become tense and yowl when they're in heat. Neutering—a surgical operation on the cat's sex organs—usually prevents these problems. For cats kept indoors it's a must. Experts suggest neutering for all cats except pedigreed animals who are being bred. This also keeps down the number of unwanted cats who are born and then abandoned.

Cats are usually neutered after they're six months old. Neutering doesn't change the cat's personality or make it get fat, but it does make the cat much pleasanter to live with.

Where should you get your cat?

A pet shop isn't the best place to get a cat. There are many ways to find free cats. Check newspapers and neighborhood bulletin boards for families and shelters offering free cats and kittens. If you want a registered cat, be sure to go to a reputable breeder.

Breeders advertise in cat magazines and local newspapers. A good way to find a breeder is to visit a cat show. It's also a good place to see a variety of breeds. Registered cats are usually expensive because of their special breeding and care. If somebody offers you a "bargain," beware! The cat may be defective in an important way.

A breeder should show you the cat's registration papers and transfer them to you. The breeder, or anyone else you pay for a cat, should also guarantee the

animal's health. The breeder should agree to let a veterinarian examine the cat and refund your money if the animal isn't healthy. Some breeders will also give you a one-year guarantee against inherited defects that show up after the cat is grown.

How do you select a cat?

Kittens should be eight weeks old before they leave their mother. Kittens younger than that probably aren't housebroken and weaned (eating solid food instead of milk).

Shy kittens may actually be sick. Be sure your kitten is lively, alert, and friendly. See if it will chase a ball of paper or a piece of string. Pick it up gently.

The kitten may claw and cling for a while, but it should relax as you comfort it. If it doesn't, that means it's always going to be nervous and fearful—not the kind of cat you want!

Be sure the kitten doesn't have a runny nose or eyes. These indicate disease. Its ears should be clean. Dirty ears often mean the kitten has ear mites, which are a nuisance to get rid of. The teeth should be white and sharp, the gums firm and muscular.

Look under the kitten's tail for worms or diarrhea. While you're looking you can check whether the kitten is male or female. A female has two openings that look like the letter "i." A male's will look like a colon (:). But unless you are an expert, you may confuse them!

Set the kitten down and clap your hands behind it. An animal that doesn't respond might be deaf.

A clean beginning is also a plus. Don't get your cat from a place that's dirty or smells too heavily of cat odors. See if your cat's littermates are healthy too. Diseases spread quickly from animal to animal.

All this may seem complicated, but it's just common sense. Unless you're looking for a super-duper show cat, chances are you'll find the perfect pet quickly. If you are choosing a grown cat, take the same kind of care.

Once you know the kitten or cat you want, find out its habits. Ask what it eats

and how often. Has it been trained to use a litter box? What kind of litter? You can change these habits in a while, but staying with what's familiar to your cat will help it adapt to its biggest change—a new home.

Be sure to ask whether the cat or kitten has had its shots, and if so, which ones.

As soon as you get your cat, take it to a vet for a checkup. The vet will tell you if the cat is basically healthy and will know what vaccinations to give it. These shots are important because they protect your cat against deadly diseases.

How do you bring your cat home?

The trip home can be very frightening for your cat. You don't want a scared kitten slipping out of your hands into the street or under the gas pedal of your car. So be sure to put it in a cat carrier—a special box with airholes and a handle. Veterinarians have cardboard carriers you can use. If you plan to travel often with your cat, you can get a wood-and-wire carrier at a pet store.

What supplies should you have for your cat?

Before you bring your new cat home, there are things you will need. The most important ones are

- two tip-proof dishes for food and water
- cat food
- a plastic or metal litter tray
- a bag of cat litter
- a slotted sifting spoon for removing waste from the tray
- some sort of bed (a shallow cardboard box and an old cushion or blanket will do)
- cat toys—ones the cat can't swallow.

Prepare your home for the new arrival! Cats are naturally agile, but they sometimes knock things over while playing. Put breakable glass where the cat can't get it. The same goes for houseplants, which many cats will nibble. Some plants are poisonous to cats. It's also a good idea to run electrical cords behind furniture so the cat can't injure itself by biting or clawing through them.

On the way home speak softly to your pet. Once you get there, set out some food and water but don't be surprised if the cat isn't in the mood to eat or drink at first. Be sure to put your cat's bed in a

warm place. Kittens are especially sensitive to cold drafts.

Put the cat in its litter box and make a few scratching motions with its front paws. This will remind it to use the litter box instead of the floor. Then let your new pet explore its new home. But keep an eye out so the cat doesn't get into trouble. Many kittens adjust to their new homes quickly—even jumping into their owners' laps right away! Others may hide behind a sofa and cry. But most cats will feel at home within a day or so. And your home will look homier too—with a kitten curled up asleep!

Give your cat plenty of affection, but don't overdo it. Kittens need lots of sleep, so try not to disturb them when they're resting. And remember, cats *are* independent. When they don't want to sit in your lap they really *don't want to.* When they *do,* enjoy it as a friendly gift to you!

CATS
Cats asleep
Anywhere,
Any table,
Any chair,
Top of piano.
Window-ledge,
In the middle,
On the edge,
Open drawer,
Empty shoe,
Anybody's
Lap will do.
Fitted in a
Cardboard box,
In the cupboard
With your frocks—
Anywhere!
They don't care!
Cats sleep
Anywhere.

—Eleanor Farjeon,
The Children's Bells

What should you feed your cat?

Cats are meat-eaters, but they can't thrive on a diet of meat alone. Wild cats eat the whole animal they catch—everything from the bones to the grass and vegetables in its stomach. Wild cats also eat greens now and then.

What should you feed your cat? Experts disagree on the best diet. They do agree that a cat's diet should be varied. Don't let your cat or kitten get used to just one type of food.

If you use commercial cat foods, look for ones that say "complete" or "balanced" on the label. Feed your cat different flavors—beef, liver, chicken, kidney—and supplement his diet with egg yolks (but not the whites), margarine, and cooked vegetables. Milk is all right now and then, but not if it gives your cat diarrhea. Cooked or canned fish is okay too, but only once a week. Too much can make a cat fatally ill.

There are some things *not* to serve your cat. Raw meats and fish can carry parasites. Chicken or turkey bones, raw or cooked, can stick in a cat's throat, so keep them away from your cat. Be careful when you throw bones away—cats are very clever at stealing them from the garbage!

Kittens should be fed at least four times a day until they're about four months old; then three times daily until six months; then twice a day until their first birthday. After that, one meal a day should be enough.

This sort of schedule can be hard for busy people to follow, so it's all right to leave food out all day and let the kitten eat whenever it chooses. If you feed your cat this way, be sure to change stale food often. Dried-up food smells bad and attracts insects. Besides, your cat doesn't like stale food any more than you do.

As cats grow older, they need less food. It's easy to leave out a bowl of dry commercial food. Some cats tend to overeat and get fat, so it's best to limit the amount of food you set out. An adult cat should maintain its weight, just like people. A fat cat is not a healthy cat!

All cats need water. Be sure there's plenty in the water dish and change it daily.

Catnip and Cats

Cats LOVE catnip–probably because of its smell. The catnip is a plant that belongs to the mint family. Give your cat a little and watch what happens! Your cat will roll around in it, looking ecstatic. Catnip makes old cats act like kittens and makes kittens act even younger. We don't know exactly <u>why</u> catnip works, but it certainly does work. Ask any cat!

What do you do about the litter box?

Cats easily learn to use the litter box. (They instinctively bury their feces so bigger animals can't trace them by the smell.) Most people leave the litter tray in the bathroom, which makes it simple to clean. Just sift out solid waste daily with the slotted spoon and flush it down the toilet. Stir up the litter to help it dry out.

When the litter becomes wet, change it. The old litter shouldn't be dumped down the toilet. That will ruin the plumbing. Instead, empty it into a paper bag and discard it in the garbage.

It's not likely to happen, but some diseases can be transmitted to humans from cat waste. Try not to touch the used litter or waste, and always wash your hands well after tending to the litter box.

How do you help groom your cat?

Cats are naturally clean, but a little help doesn't hurt. Brushing your cat helps keep it from swallowing too much hair and vomiting up hairballs. And the fur you collect on your brush won't collect on the furniture! Your cat should get used to regular brushing while it's still a kitten.

Cats usually don't need baths, which is just as well, because most cats hate water. If your cat should become caked with mud or roll in grease, it's best to wipe off what you can and ask the vet for advice about bathing.

Trimming the cat's front claws will help keep it from scratching you too deeply if it gets carried away playing. You can use a nail clipper or an animal-claw clipper. Be careful not to cut into the pink area of the nail. This has a blood vessel that will bleed and be very painful to your cat—and discourage it from enduring any more nail-cutting.

Cats <u>Can</u> Learn To

fetch
come when their names
   are called
jump through a hoop
shake hands
lie down
roll over
use a cat door
use the toilet
swim
sit up and box
walk on a leash.

How do you train your cat?

Cats and kittens need lots of love and plenty of play. The more situations your cat learns to cope with as a kitten, the calmer it will be as an adult meeting new adventures.

There are many safe toys you can buy. Be sure to stay away from strings or rubber bands, which can be fatal if swallowed!

Kittens *can* be trained. If they're doing something they shouldn't, shout "No!" and give them a tap on the nose. Soon your kitten will learn what's expected of it. Eventually it will respond to "No!" and not need the tap at all.

Cats must scratch off the rough edges of their claws, and they often use carpets, drapes, and furniture for this. You can solve this problem by making or buying a carpet-covered scratching post and putting some catnip on it. The post should be tall enough so your cat can stretch out to its full length while scratching at it.

Every time you see your cat scratching where it shouldn't, take it to the post and make scratching motions with its front legs. If you begin this from kittenhood and keep the cat's nails trimmed, you may never have a problem.

But some cats never learn, scratching wherever they please. Vets can operate on cats to remove their claws, but they

disagree about whether or not it should be done. All vets agree that it's wrong to declaw a cat that roams outdoors. If it should run into an enemy, the cat wouldn't be able to use its claws to defend itself or scramble up a tree.

Some people say declawing is cruel and makes the cat distrustful of people. Recovery from the operation can also be painful. People in favor of the operation say that cats can adjust if they're declawed before the age of six months. Declawing may be the only solution for a cat that keeps ruining the furniture.

Should your cat go outside?

Some cats live indoors all their lives. Others are allowed to roam outdoors when they feel like it. If you live in a city or town, you should keep your cat inside.

Speeding cars and trucks, poisons, and numerous other dangers are constant threats to a cat's life.

Country Barnyard

Cats and kittens, kittens and cats
under the barn and under the shed;
a face by the steps, a tail by the ramp
and off they go, if they hear a tread!

Sleep in the sun with one eye on guard,
doze in the grass with a listening ear,
run for the darkness under the barn
as soon as a human being draws near!

Not quite wild and not quite tame,
thin and limber, with hungry eye:
the house cat sits at the kitchen door
disdainfully watching her kin go by.

—Elizabeth Coatsworth
Night and the Cat

In the suburbs and the country cats may be allowed to roam free. If they do they should be neutered so they won't add more kittens to the millions of those already unwanted.

Even in the country an outdoor cat faces many dangers an indoor cat doesn't. Indoor cats tend to stay healthier and live longer than their free-roaming relatives.

THE ALLEY CAT SCROUNGES FOR FOOD

HE POKES HIS HEAD INTO A PROMISING GARBAGE CAN

PEEEYEWWW!

Do cats get sick?

Just like people, cats get sick now and then. But cats can't tell you how they're feeling. A detailed cat-health book like the ones listed on page 88 can help you determine what's wrong with your cat. Here are a few signals to watch for:

A change in behavior   When cats get sick, they often become less active. Sometimes they go into a corner and don't move at all. Some illnesses make a cat run wildly. Call a vet if your cat goes to any of these extremes for a day or so.

A change of appetite   When cats get sick, they often refuse to eat or drink. Sometimes they'll eat less or more than usual. If your cat avoids food or water for more than a day or two, call the vet.

Humanlike symptoms of illness
Cats sometimes sneeze, vomit, and display a variety of ailments from runny eyes to diarrhea. These symptoms aren't always serious; often they disappear by themselves. But when they last more than two or three days or go along with a change of appetite or behavior, consult your vet.

Emergencies   If your cat is involved in an accident, wrap it in a heavy blanket to keep it warm (and to keep it from clawing you out of fear). Then rush it to the vet. If there's heavy bleeding, try to control it by holding a bandage or any piece of cloth firmly against the wound until you can get help.

IMPORTANT!

Aspirin is poisonous to cats. So are most other medicines that people take. Never give them to a cat or a kitten unless a vet tells you to do so.

Minor ailments   Probably the most common problems in cat health are parasites—tiny animals that live on or in a cat's body.

Fleas are tiny, dark-brown insects that live by sucking blood from the skin of a dog or cat—or human. Many antiflea products are available. Use only those that are safe for cats, and be sure to follow the directions carefully.

Various worms can live in your cat's intestines. Some are invisible, but some may look like grains of rice in your cat's feces. If you think your cat has worms, call your vet and use only the medicines he or she recommends.

Cat Shows

The first modern cat show was held in 1871 at London's Crystal Palace. Ten years later the idea spread to America. Today there are more than three hundred cat shows each year in North America.

Cat shows have two types of competitions. Pedigreed cats without major flaws enter the *championship* category. These are the only cats that can win the title "Champion." All other cats—from purebred animals with defects to ordinary household pets—must compete in the *non-championship* class.

Sick cats can't be shown. A vet usually checks each cat before it's allowed into the show hall. Inside, the cats wait their turn in cages decorated with the ribbons they've won before. When it's time for competition, each cat is taken to a plain cage in the judging ring.

The judges are all cat experts and have gone through a special training program. They know the standard for every breed in the show. They've also bred champions themselves.

The judges study each contestant and

award the cat a score based on how close it comes to the standard for its breed.

A cat that wins in the first ring can go on to win more awards. Many prizes are given in each show. Some say "Second Best Siamese" or "Best Longhair." But the prize every registered cat-owner wants is the dark-blue ribbon with the simple inscription: "BEST CAT"!

Prize cats at the Crystal Palace Cat Show, 1871

Cat Names

"The Naming of Cats is a difficult matter," wrote the poet T. S. Eliot. And no wonder! Would Garfield be the same if he'd been named Snookie-Poo Cuddleums the Third?

The Cat Fancy insists that no two pedigreed animals can have the same name. That's why an official registered cat name can look like this: Ambergrain's Mugwump of Nickandjenny. You'd probably call this cat Mugwump for short. The first part of his name says he was bred at the Ambergrain cattery, and the last part lets you know he now belongs to the Nickandjenny cattery.

Most cats' names are a lot simpler. Mark Twain kept eleven cats at one time. He called one of them Bags. But the others were Danbury, Buffalo Bill, Pestilence, Famine, Sackcloth, Ashes, Satan, Sin, Blatherskite, and Beelzebub! It must have sounded wild when he called them!

An English poet named Robert Southey had a cat with these titles: The Most Noble, the Archduke Rumpelstiltskin, Marcus Macbum, Earl Tomlefagne, Baron Raticide, Waowhler and Scratch!

Around the house he was just called Rumpel.

There's a man in Massachusetts who has a dog named Cat and a cat named Dog. What a confusing home that must be!

Get to know your kitten before you name it. Is it a Prince? Or simply a Puss? Does it have a distinctive color marking? Does it *do* something unusual or *look* like somebody? Or do you just like the sound of a name like Sweetpea? Remember: your cat will be stuck with its name *forever*. So name it with love!

White House Cats

Abe Lincoln's son Tad had a cat named Tabby. Theodore Roosevelt had a cat named Slippers. Gerald Ford's daughter Susan had a Siamese cat named Shem. The first Siamese cat to appear in this country was sent as a gift to President Rutherford B. Hayes.

Cats at Work

Millions of cats like Garfield are house pets whose biggest job may be to meow for their supper! But many other cats really do work for a living.

Salty Cats

For centuries sailors wouldn't consider sailing on a ship without a mouser aboard. They rid the ship of pesty mice and rats—and they never got seasick.

Post Office Cats

The British Post Office keeps cats to guard against rats and mice. Over the years these working cats have earned salaries to pay for the food they eat.

Farm Cats

Micky, a farmer's cat in Lancaster, England, killed one thousand mice a year—for twenty-three years!

Shop Cats

In the United States working cats are the unofficial Rodent Control Department for butcher shops, fish markets, grocery stores—even for art galleries and television stations!

Seeing-eye Cats

A blind woman in California had a seeing-eye cat. In one year he learned how to walk on a leash, touch his tail against her legs at corners, and pull on his leash when it was safe to cross the street. He also signaled steps going up or down.

Hearing Cats

Impy and Hinky lived with a deaf woman in Idaho. She would set her alarm clock at night, and when it went off in the morning, her cats would hear it and wake her with their paws. They would also lead her to the kitchen when a pot boiled over. If someone came to visit, her clever cats would touch her on the foot to tell her.

THE ACTOR CAT IS BEING FILMED ESCAPING FROM THE ENEMY

CATS' PENCHANT FOR SHARPEN-
ING THEIR CLAWS HAS SERVED
MANY HISTORIC PURPOSES:
IN VICTORIAN TIMES CATS WERE
USED TO ANTIQUE FURNITURE

DURING THE SPANISH-AMERICAN
WAR, CATS WERE USED AS
INTERROGATORS

I'LL TALK!
I'LL TALK!

AND TODAY, THE POST OFFICE
USES CATS TO SORT MAIL
MARKED "FRAGILE"

Sales Cat

Of course, everybody knows about Morris the Cat, a big orange tom who sold cat food on television. There are other cats who appear on cat food boxes and cans. Occasionally there are contests for house cats. Who knows—even your own cat may become a star!

Astro Cat

A tabby named Felicette was the most unusual working cat in the universe. In 1962 she rode a French rocket nearly one hundred miles into space. Felicette was the world's only feline astronaut. (Unless you count Leo the Lion, a constellation in the sky!)

ALMOST MAKES
ME WISH I HAD
A JOB

STORE HOURS
8·6

 **Cat Proverbs**

The cat likes fish,
but won't wet his feet.

At night all cats are gray.

(Because you can't see colors in the dark.)

When the cat's away,
the mice will play.

56

Curiosity killed the cat.

Honest as a cat when the meat is out of reach.

(The only time you can *really* trust it.)

There's more than one way to skin a cat.

(More than one way to do something.)

A cat has nine lives.

(Because it seems to get out of so many scrapes without hurting itself.)

 **True Cat Tales**

The Fishing Cat

In seventeenth-century Paris, the river Seine often flooded its banks in the spring. Cellars filled with water and many hungry people went fishing in them.

One clever cat went down to a cellar and scooped up fish with a swipe of its paw!

He became so popular that Parisians named a street in his honor. It's called the *Rue du Chat-qui-Pêche*—the street of the fishing cat. The street is still there—three hundred years later.

The Cat in Room 8

One day in 1953 a hungry gray-and-white tomcat wandered into the Elysian Heights Elementary School in Los Angeles. When students in room 8 fed him scraps of their lunches, he decided to visit regularly.

The students named him Room 8. He never missed a day of school!

There was a book written about him and he appeared on television. Over ten thousand people wrote letters to him, and the sixth grade students answered them all, signing them with a special paw-print stamp.

Room 8 died in 1968 after fifteen years as the school's most faithful student. A hospital fund for sick children was named after him.

A Cat at Sea

William Willis, an explorer, traveled seven hundred miles on a raft—with only a parrot and a cat. Who *says* cats and birds can't get along?

Sugar, the Terrific Traveler

Sugar, a tomcat, lived in Anderson, California. When his owners moved, they left him behind with neighbors. Fourteen months later Sugar arrived at the new home of his old owner—fifteen hundred miles away in Gage, Oklahoma! He probably did it by using his keen sense of smell.

High-flying Cat

A Siamese named Sherry did enough traveling to last nine lifetimes. She was lost in the cargo area of a jetliner when her owners moved from Guam to San Francisco in 1979. Sherry was found on the plane thirty-two days later, skinny and hurt but still alive. She had gone to 12 countries and flown 225,000 miles!

Life-saving Cat

Once there was a farmer who was too ill and too poor to buy meat. His cat saved his life by bringing him a bird or a rabbit each day.

War Hero

During World War Two a Russian cat named Mourka showed great bravery. He crossed a street through gunfire to carry soldiers' messages from the battlefield to headquarters.

Simon, the Ship's Cat

Simon was a navy cat whose ship ran aground on a Chinese island. When rats clambered aboard, Simon fought them off. He did this for three months until his ship could set sail again. At home Simon became the first cat to win the Dickin Medal—England's highest award for animal heroism.

Rich Cats

Dr. William Grier's pets, Hellcat and Brownie, became the wealthiest cats ever. When Dr. Grier died, he left them his entire fortune—$415,000.

Squatter's Rights

Listen, Kitten,
Get this clear;
This is my chair.
I sit here.

Okay, Kitty,
We can share;
When I'm not home,
It's your chair.

Listen, Tom Cat,
How about
If I use it
When you're out?

—Richard Shaw,
The Cat Book

Very Clever Cat

This cat in Melbourne Beach, Florida, was such an enthusiastic surfer that his owner bought him his own surfboard.

Fat Cat

Joseph, a cat in England, is famous for his size. He weighs forty-eight pounds. A large bequest left to him by his owner made Joseph a wealthy fat cat.

♪ MERORRR

Cat Language

♫ ROWERROWER ♪

Caterwaul
  yowl or screech
  like a cat

Catnap   a short sleep

FRED'S FRESH FISH

Catfish   a type of
  fish with
  whiskers

Cattail   a plant that grows in marshes

Catbird   a mockingbird with a catlike
  cry

Catkin   a spike of flowers that looks like
  a cat's tail

Pussy willow   a small tree with furry
  catkins

TAPPITY
TAPPITY
TAPPITY

Catwalk
  a narrow walkway

Copycat   an imitator

Pussyfoot
  avoid making
  a decision

Cool cat   a person who's calm and hip

Fat cat
  a wealthy person

The cat's pajamas
  something first-rate

Catboat   a type of small sailboat

POOF!

PEROWRR ♫

CHUKONG!

Cat's cradle a game played with string

Scaredy cat a fearful person

Cat-o'-nine-tails a lash

Cat burglar a thief who climbs walls quietly

Cat's got his tongue he won't answer

Let the cat out of the bag give away a secret

Rain cats and dogs rain heavily

Fight like cats and dogs argue violently

Live a cat-and-dog life have lots of trouble

Look like the cat that swallowed the canary have a wonderful secret you're not telling

"Cats" Around the World

How do you say "cat" in foreign languages? Here are a few of the ways:

French: *chat*
German: *katze*
Swedish: *katt*
Spanish: *gato*
Arabic: *qit*
Chinese: *mao*
Russian: *koshka*
Persian: *pushak*
Japanese: *neko*
Dutch: *kat*
Romanian: *pisicca*
Armenian: *kitta*
Italian: *gatto*
Polish: *kot*

GARFIELD'S HISTORY OF CATS: A CAT DISCOVERED AMERICA!

IT WAS CHRISTOPHER COLUMBUS' CAT "BUCKEYE" WHO FIRST SPOTTED THE BEACH

PRIMARILY BECAUSE THE SANTA MARIA DIDN'T HAVE A SANDBOX

Half Asleep

To assume a cat's asleep
is a grave mistake.
He can close his eyes and keep
both his ears *awake.*

—Aileen Fisher,
My Cat Has Eyes of Sapphire Blue

Cats in Art

Some of the world's greatest artists have painted or drawn cats. In a Goya portrait two cats stare—eagerly—at a boy's pet bird. A picture by Manet shows two very mysterious cats meeting on a rooftop under the moon. Picasso painted bird-hunting cats and fat, contented cats. Well-known artists such as Gainsborough, Renoir, Chagall, Rousseau, Gauguin, and Cassat included cats in their works.

House Cats

Francisco de Goya

Auguste Renoir

Jean Antoine Watteau

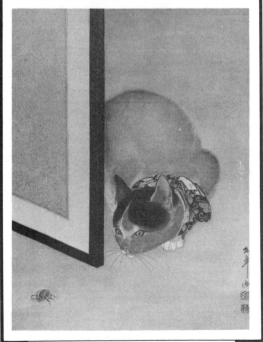

Japanese Painting on Silk

Edouard Manet

Early American Painting

Paul Davis

Alexandre Theophile Steinlen

Cat Photos

Cats are fun to photograph too.
People buy many books each year
to look at unusual and beautiful cats.
Everybody who has a cat sooner or
later *has* to take a picture of it!

Cats have brightened the mails in several countries. In 1965 Poland, Romania, and Yemen issued postage stamps with portraits of European, Persian, and Siamese cats. A Yugoslavian stamp used a fanciful cat to celebrate Children's Week.

A cat, two dogs, and a boy were shown in a 1957 Cuban stamp honoring their humane society. A man with a microscope and a child with an Angora cat appeared on a 1967 stamp celebrating the 125th anniversary of Turkish veterinary medicine.

The Isle of Man honored its Manx cat with a stamp in 1973. And a 1968 stamp from Poland featured the fairy-tale cat Puss-in-Boots.

But the United States has never had a cat stamp!

DYRENES BESKYTTELSE
90
DANMARK

STATE OF OMAN
Postage 5b
Siamese Seal-Pointed

100
POSTE AÉRIEN
RÉPUBLIQUE DU TCHAD

55 BANI
Posta Romănă

MAGYAR POSTA

STATE OF OMAN
Airmail 2b
Manx Cat

GR
40
Polska

75 BANI
Posta Romănă

POSTAGE
3 BAHT
ประเทศไทย THAILAND
SIAMESE CAT   PURE WHITE

PARAGUAY
₲0.10

STATE OF OMAN
Postage 12b
Long Haired Blue Cream

Cat Coins

A few coins from ancient times showed cats on them. In modern times cats have only been featured on the 1970 one-crown piece and the 1975 twenty-five-pence coin from the Isle of Man. Each coin shows the profile of Queen Elizabeth II on one side and the island's native Manx cat on the other.

 # *Cats in Folklore*

Cats have played an important part in the customs and beliefs of people all over the world.

In Egypt and elsewhere cats were considered kind gods. Freya, the Scandinavian goddess of beauty and love, traveled in a chariot pulled by cats. But in Roman mythology the cat was likened to Hecate, goddess of the underworld.

Sometimes the cat was seen as evil. Witches were believed to take on the form of cats, and vice versa. Black cats were sacrificed to the Devil in some European ceremonies.

Some people thought cats had supernatural powers. In the Middle Ages a live cat was sometimes imprisoned within the walls of a new house to protect it from witches. In Japan people said that bewitched cats played with balls of fire and spoke human languages.

Different breeds of cats were thought to bring good or bad luck. Sailors and landlubbers used cat behavior to predict

a storm. Calicos were considered especially good for this. This may be more than just a superstition. The cat's sensitive fur makes it notice changes in barometric pressure—and these changes are often what precedes a storm.

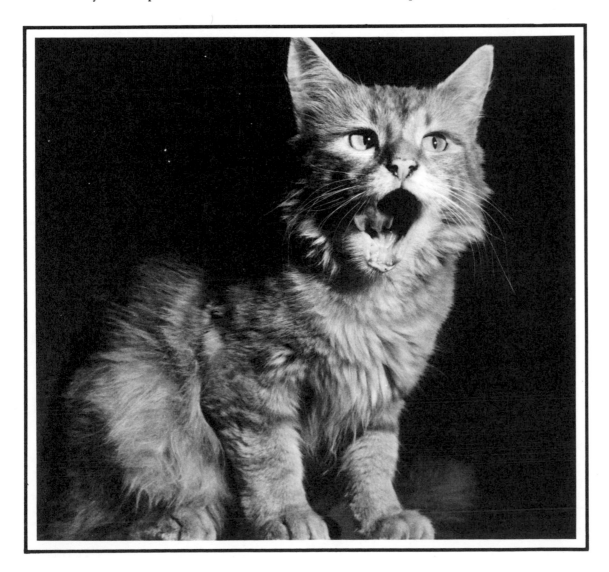

Cat Superstitions

All sorts of superstitions about cats have sprung up over time. Here are a few:

If a black cat crosses your path, you'll have bad luck.
—United States

A black cat will bring good luck.
—England and Scotland

A white cat will bring good luck.
—United States

Three-colored cats bring good luck.
—Japan and Canada

Kiss the black cat,
and 'twill make you fat.
Kiss the white one,
and 'twill make you lean.
—England

When the cat washes her face, it's a sign of rain.
—Scotland

When the cat washes her face, it's a sign of fair weather.
—England and United States

Cats born in May bring snakes to the house.
—Wales

If you swallow a cat's hair, you will die.
—England

To keep a cat at home, butter its paws.
—United States

If you cut off a cat's whiskers, it will lose its sense of smell.
—United States

Cats have nine lives.
—Many countries

Famous Cartoon Cats

Krazy Kat

Felix the Cat

A CAT WHO LIKES MICKEY MOUSE

GARFIELD!

Puss-in-Boots, illustrated by Gustave Doré

Myths and Folk Tales About Cats

There are lots of myths and folk tales about clever cats.

A cat in *Aesop's Fables* keeps threatening the lives of the mice. They decide that the only way to protect themselves is to put a bell around the cat's neck to warn them when he's coming. But there's one problem: *Who* is going to tie the bell on? This fable shows that in trying to solve *one* problem you may end up with another!

In another fable a fox brags that if dogs attack him he can escape in a hundred different ways. The cat says she knows just one. When a pack of hounds does attack, the cat scrambles up a tree to safety, but the fox is so busy deciding which tricks to use that the dogs quickly catch him.

Probably the all-time champion is Puss-in-Boots. He outwits rabbits, foxes, ogres, and kings—and wins a castle and a princess for his poor but kindly master. Many artists have painted Puss-in-Boots looking very dapper in his fancy outfits!

According to one Arab legend the original pair of mice on Noah's Ark kept having babies. Noah got desperate with so many mice around. Finally he asked a lioness to help him. And she did—by sneezing a pair of cats!

A Chinese story says cats are dignified and playful because the first cat's mother was a lioness—and its father was a monkey!

A fable of Aesop, illustrated by Grandville

Why Do Cats Wash After Meals?

According to a Turkish legend a cat caught a sparrow and was just about to eat it when the sparrow said, "Brother Cat, don't you know you should always wash before dinner?" The proud cat was embarrassed to hear this because he always thought himself so clean. So he let go of the sparrow and began to wash his hands. Instantly the clever sparrow flew away! And from then on the cat, learning his lesson, washes himself only after meals.

How Did Manx Cats Lose Their Tails?

One legend says that they were dawdling as they went up the ramp to the Ark. Noah shut the door on their tails before they got inside.

Why Do Some Cats Have Kinky Tails?

An old cat tale says it goes back to a time when a cat's job was to guard a sacred goblet. He couldn't stay awake all day and all night, so he wrapped his tail around the goblet to protect it. When his mission was over, his tail had a permanent curly kink. And so, now, do his descendants' tails.

Who Was Dick Whittington?

Dick Whittington was a boy who worked for a rich merchant in London. One day the merchant offered to help his poorer employees by trading goods for them abroad. Dick Whittington had only one thing he could send—his cat.

Months passed, and Dick was lonely without his cat. He gave up hope for any success and set out for his old country village. But on Allhallows Day, the church bells in the country suddenly began ringing. They seemed to be saying: "Turn again, Whittington, Thrice Lord Mayor of London." Dick returned to London and discovered he had become rich! His cat had valiantly killed the rats in the palace of a faraway king. The king was impressed and bought the cat—for gold, jewels, and silks.

Is this story true? No one can say. But there was a real Dick Whittington who became a wealthy merchant around 1400. And just as the bells in the story promised, he was elected Lord Mayor of London three times!

How Did the Cat Get Its Purr?

According to a tale from France a beautiful princess was told to spin ten thousand balls of linen in a month. If she failed, the prince she loved would die.

The princess had three white cats who were very clever. They spun the fiber into thread for her on the spinning wheels, and their hard work saved the prince!

At the couple's wedding feast the cats were guests of honor. They curled up contentedly and began humming just like spinning wheels. The purr was a gift they were given for helping the princess. And so cats still purr to this day.

Cats in Literature

How many books and stories are there about cats? Enough to fill many bookshelves! Fictional cats appear in many funny—and frightening—tales.

The Cat in the Hat
© 1957 by Dr. Seuss

Rudyard Kipling wrote about *The Cat That Walked by Himself*. "He will kill mice and he will be kind to babies when he is in the house, just so long as they do not pull his tail too hard. But when he has done that, and between times, he is the Cat that walks by himself, and all places are alike to him....He goes out to the Wet Wild Woods...waving his wild tail and walking by his wild lone."

Don Marquis wrote about a fun-loving cat named Mehitabel who tells the story of her many lives to a clever cockroach named Archie, who can type it for her! In *Jennie*, by Paul Gallico, a boy turns into a cat. And in Edgar Allan Poe's *The Black Cat*, a one-eyed feline's howl reveals a murderer.

Many cats have popped up in books for children. Everybody knows the Cheshire Cat in Lewis Carroll's *Alice's Adventures in Wonderland*, who often fades into thin air—except for his big grin, which disappears last. Beatrix Potter's Tom Kitten gets tied up by rats and rolled into a "roly-poly pudding." In Wanda Gag's *Millions of Cats*, "hundreds and thousands and millions and billions and trillions of cats" get into a fight over which one is the prettiest. And Dr. Seuss's mischievous *Cat in the Hat* has helped to teach many many children how to read.

There is a book of funny poems about

cats written by T. S. Eliot. It's called *Old Possum's Book of Practical Cats*. And the British poet Thomas Gray wrote a poem with the saddest title you ever heard: "On the Death of a Favorite Cat, Drowned in a Tub of Gold Fishes."

You can find books about cats in your library. The Glendale, California, public library probably has whatever you are looking for: it has a special collection of more than fifteen hundred volumes about cats.

Alice's Adventures in Wonderland was written by Lewis Carroll in 1865. This illustration of Alice and the Cheshire Cat was drawn by Sir John Tenniel for the first edition.

Alley Cat School

Do alley cats go
    to alley cat school?
Where they learn how to slink
    and stay out of sight?
Where they learn how to find
    warm and comfortable places,
On a cold wintry night?
Do they learn from teachers and books
    how to topple a garbage can lid?
Did they all go
    to alley cat school?
Is that what they did?

              —Frank Asch,
              City Sandwich

Cat Quotes

"God made the cat to give man
the pleasure of petting the tiger."
                    –François Méry

"If you want to . . . write about
human beings, the best thing you
can do is keep a pair of cats."
                    –Aldous Huxley

WHAT DO YOU GET
IF YOU CROSS A
CAT AND A DOG?

> *"When I play with my cat, who knows whether I do not make her more sport than she makes me? . . . Perhaps she laughs at my simplicity in making sport to amuse her."*
>
> *—Michel de Montaigne*

> *"If man could be crossed with the cat it would improve man, but it would deteriorate the cat."*
>
> *—Mark Twain*

More About Cats

If you'd like to read more about cats, here are some excellent books to try:

Cat Care

McGinniss, Terri. *The Well Cat Book*. Random House, 1975.

Whitney, Leon F., and George D. Whitney. *The Complete Book of Cat Care*. Doubleday, 1980.

The Basic Cat

Beadle, Muriel. *The Cat*. Simon and Schuster, 1977.

Fox, Michael. *Understanding Your Cat*. Coward, 1974.

Cat Breeds

Gebhardt, Richard H., and others. *A Standard Guide to Cat Breeds*. McGraw-Hill, 1979.

Cats in General

Fireman, Judy, ed. *Cat Catalog*. Workman, 1976.

Necker, Claire. *The Natural History of Cats*. Dell, 1977.

Necker, Claire. *The Complete Cat*. Simon and Schuster, 1980.

Cat Stories, Poems, and Art

Alexander, Lloyd. *The Cat Who Wished to Be a Man*. Dutton, 1972.

Averill, Esther. *Jenny and the Cat Club*. Harper & Row, 1973.

Bonsall, Crosby and Ylla. *I'll Show You Cats*. Harper & Row, 1964.

Byars, Betsy. *Rama, the Gypsy Cat*. Avon, 1976.

Calhoun, Mary. *The House of Thirty Cats*. Archway, 1965.

Chenery, Janet. *Pickles and Jake*. Viking-Penguin, 1975.

Estes, Eleanor. *Pinky Pie*. Harcourt Brace Jovanovich, 1976.

Hildick, E. W. *The Case of the Condemned Cat*. Archway, 1978.

Leach, Maria. *The Lion Sneezed: Folktales and Myths of the Cat*. Crowell, 1977.

MacBeth, George, and Martin Booth, eds. *The Book of Cats*. Morrow, 1977.

Manley, Seon, and Gogo Lewis, eds. *Cat Encounters*. Lothrop, 1977.

Sargeant, Sarah. *Edward Troy and the Witch Cat*. Follett, 1978.

Seuss, Dr. *The Cat in the Hat*. Random House, 1957.

Seuss, Dr. *The Cat in the Hat Comes Back*. Random House, 1958.

Suares, Jean-Claude, and Seymour Chwast, eds. *The Literary Cat*. Putnam, 1977.

Index